# 1·2·3 Phonics

## Grades PreK–K

Published by Totline® Publications
an imprint of
**Frank Schaffer Publications®**

Author: Gayle Bittinger
Editor: Jeanine Manfro

**Frank Schaffer Publications®**

Totline® Publications is an imprint of Frank Schaffer Publications.

Printed in the United States of America. All rights reserved. Limited Reproduction Permission: Permission to duplicate these materials is limited to the person for whom they are purchased. Reproduction for an entire school or school district is unlawful and strictly prohibited. Frank Schaffer Publications is an imprint of School Specialty Publishing. Copyright © 2004 School Specialty Publishing.

Send all inquiries to:
Frank Schaffer Publications
8720 Orion Place
Columbus, Ohio 43240-2111

*1•2•3 Phonics*—grades PreK-K

ISBN: 1-57029-470-4

2 3 4 5 6 7 8 9 10 PAT 10 09 08 07 06

# Table of Contents

Introduction ................. 5

## The Letters of the Alphabet

| | |
|---|---|
| Aa | 6 |
| Bb | 8 |
| Cc | 10 |
| Dd | 12 |
| Ee | 14 |
| Ff | 16 |
| Gg | 18 |
| Hh | 20 |
| Ii | 22 |
| Jj | 24 |
| Kk | 26 |
| Ll | 28 |
| Mm | 30 |
| Nn | 32 |
| Oo | 34 |
| Pp | 36 |
| Qq | 38 |
| Rr | 40 |
| Ss | 42 |
| Tt | 44 |
| Uu | 46 |
| Vv | 48 |
| Ww | 50 |
| Xx | 52 |
| Yy | 54 |
| Zz | 56 |

## Alphabet Fun from A to Z .................. 58–66

A to Z
Alphabet Concentration
Alphabet Books
In the Alphabet
I Love the Alphabet
Letter Collages
Alpha-Ball
Make-Your-Own
   Alphabet Books
Alphabet Towers
Typing Letters
Letter Stencils
Modeling Clay Letters
Salt Writing
Fingerpaint Letters
Chalkboard Fun
Fill in the Blanks
Back and Forth
Roll a Category
Letters to My Friends
Letters Around the Room
Alphabet Minis
Stamping Through
   the Alphabet
Letter Sound Song
Sign Language Alphabet

## Alphabet Patterns

Rhyme Patterns ..................... 67
Cake Pattern ....................... 68
Fish Pattern ....................... 69
Kite Pattern ....................... 70
Laundry Pattern .................... 71
Sailboat Pattern ................... 72
Umbrella Pattern ................... 73
Alphabet Card Patterns .. 74–80

# Introduction

1•2•3 Phonics is designed as a resource for helping young children learn about alphabet letters and sounds. The skill-building activities in this book invite children to explore letters—what they look like; how to write them; and the sounds they make. Both cooperative and individual learning are encouraged through the hands-on art, language, music, movement, and learning games on these pages.

In 1•2•3 Phonics, you will find a unit for each letter of alphabet. Each unit contains plus ideas for introducing young children to the look, feel, and sound of the letter. In addition, there is a chapter devoted to incorporating phonics learning into all curriculum areas. You will also find time-saving patterns for making your own alphabet flash cards and other alphabet activities.

As you work with the units in this book, you will find that opportunities for learning about alphabet letters are everywhere. Feel free to take advantage of these opportunities, incorporating your own ideas, and encouraging the children to explore the world of letters around them. With 1•2•3 Phonics as a resource, you can help make their learning of the letters and sounds, an adventure of fun and discovery.

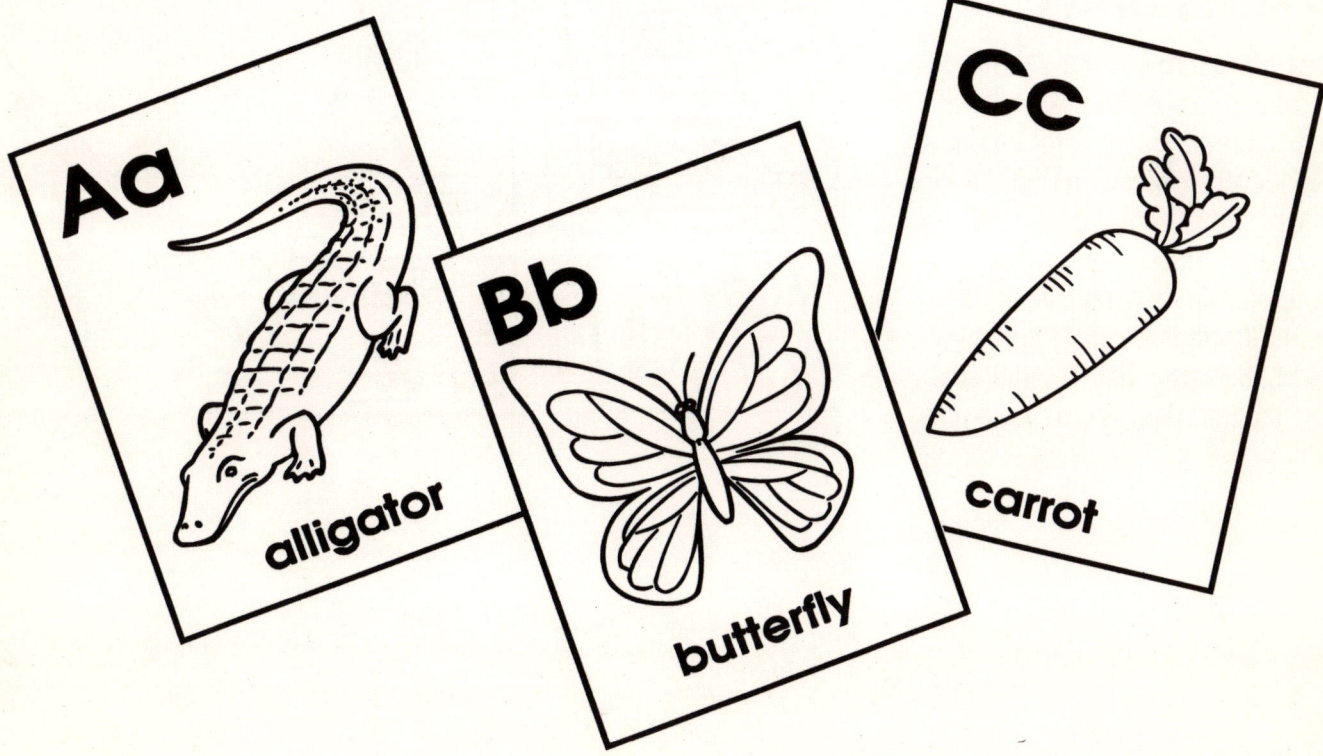

## Phonics

# Aa

## Ant A's

Give each child an *A*-shape cut out of construction paper. Set out a black, washable ink pad. Show the children how to press their fingers onto the ink pad and then onto their *A*'s, making three prints in a row to make an "ant." Have them use fine-tip black markers to add six legs to each ant. Let the children cover their *A*'s with ant prints. Hang the children's ant *A*'s all around your room.

## A Is for Apples

Cut an apple tree shape out of green felt. Cut twenty apple shapes out of red felt. Using a permanent marker, write the letter *A* on ten of the apple shapes and other letters on the remaining apples. Place the tree shape on a flannelboard and arrange the apple shapes beside it. Let the children take turns finding the apple shapes with the letter *A* on them and placing them on the apple tree.

## An Atlas of A's

Enlarge maps that show places and cities whose names begin with the letter *A*. Give each child a map. Have the children look at the maps carefully to find the letter *A*'s. Ask the children to circle all of the *A*'s that they find on their maps. Staple the children's maps together to make an atlas of *A*'s.

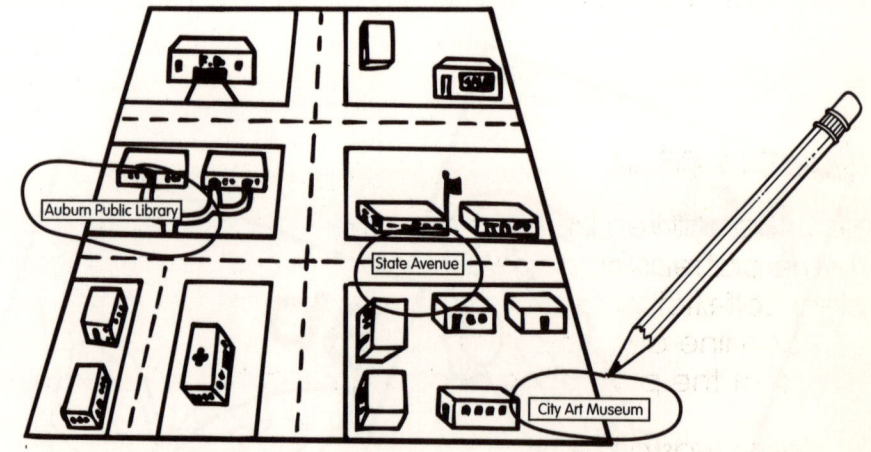

## Add an A

Set out a large sheet of paper and place a box of markers or crayons nearby. Let the children take turns writing *A's* on the paper. Encourage the children to write upper- and lowercase *A's* and to use a variety of colors.

## Acrobatic A's

Let your children discover ways to make *A's* with their bodies. Can they make an *A* with their fingers or arms? Can two children work together to make an *A*? How about three children? Can everyone work together to make one giant letter *A*?

## Ask About A's

Ask one of the children a question about an object whose name begins with *A*. For example, you could say, "I'm asking Katie about ants. Do you like ants?" or "I'm asking Wayne about apples. What kind of apple do you like?" Then let the children think of their own *A* questions to ask.

## Sound of A

Help the children begin to hear the short *a* sound in the middle of words. Photocopy the rhyme patterns on page 67. Color the patterns and laminate them (or cover them with clear self-stick paper). As you read the following rhyme to the children, pause at the end of each line and hold up the appropriate pattern. Encourage the children to say the name of the picture, emphasizing the short *a* sound in the middle.

There was a little cat
Who wore a little hat.
Her best friend was a bat.
She had a nice, soft mat.
She loved to get a pat
When she sat on her mat.

## Bb

### Beady B's

Give each child a *B*-shape cut out of construction paper. Set out glue, paintbrushes, and bowls of beads in beautiful colors. Have the children brush glue all over their letter *B's*, then let them arrange beads on their *B's* however they like. If you wish, encourage them to make patterns with their beads. Can they use the beads to make smaller letter *B's* on their big letter *B* shapes? Hang the children's beady *B's* around the room or on a bulletin board.

### Bubble B's

In a small plastic container, mix one part tempera paint with two parts liquid dishwashing detergent. Use a permanent marker to write upper- and lowercase *B's* on large sheets of plain paper. Hang one of the papers on an easel. Show the children how to dip a bubble wand into the paint and soap mixture, and then blow the paint bubbles onto the paper on the easel. The bubbles pop, leaving their prints behind.

### Big B

Use bright, fluorescent surveyors' tape (available at hardware stores) or masking tape to outline a large uppercase *B* and a lowercase *b* on the floor. Make two letter cards, one with an uppercase *B* and one with a lowercase *b*. Ask the children to stand by the letters on the floor. When you hold up the uppercase *B* card, have them stand on the uppercase *B* on the floor. When you hold up the lowercase *B* card, have the children stand on the lowercase *B*.

Phonics

## All Aboard the B Bus

Tell the children that they can go for a ride on the *B* Bus as long as they have their tickets ready. Give each child an index card. Have the children write the letter *B* on their cards and stand around the room. Pretend to be the driver, driving your bus to all the bus stops and picking up all the people that have *B* tickets.

 *Variation:* To make the game more challenging, have the children write an upper- and lowercase *B* on their tickets.

## Book of B's

Give each child a sheet of paper. Have the children write an upper- and lowercase *B* at the tops of their papers. Then let the children draw simple pictures of objects whose names begin with *B*, such as a ball, a banana, or a boat. Help them write the names of their objects at the bottom of their papers. Staple the pages together to make your group's book of *B's*.

## Bounce for B's

Give each child a bouncing ball. Stand in a large open area so that everyone has room to bounce their balls. Ask the children to listen carefully while you say a word. Have the children bounce their balls whenever they hear a word that begins with *B*.

## The Letter B

Sing the following song with the children. Let the children think of other *B* words to substitute for the word *butterfly* in the song.

Sung to: "The Muffin Man"

I'm thinking of the letter *B,*
The letter *B,* the letter *B.*
I'm thinking of the letter *B.*
Butterfly begins with *B.*

## Phonics

# Cc

## Cotton C's

Give each child a C-shape cut out of construction paper. Set out bowls of glue and cotton balls. Show the children how to dip cotton balls into the glue and then place them on their letter *C's*. Have the children cover their letter shapes with cotton. When the children's letters are finished, hang all them around your room.

## Count the C Cookies

Cut twenty cookie shapes out of brown construction paper. Write the letter *C* on ten of the cookie shapes and other letters on the remaining cookies. Mix up the cookie shapes and place them in a container. Set out a cookie sheet. Let one child take a cookie out of the container. If it has a letter *C* written on it, have the child place it on the cookie sheet. If it has a different letter written on it, have the child put the cookie back into the container. Continue until all of the *C* cookies have been found.

## C Is for Camera

Give one of the children a nonworking camera. Let the child use the camera to take pretend pictures of all the letter *C's* in your room. If necessary, write upper- and lowercase *C's* on index cards and place them in strategic places around the room.

## Collage of C's

Hang a length of butcher paper on the wall at the children's eye level. Set out a variety of writing instruments, such as markers, pencils, colored pencils, paint and paintbrushes, pastels, and watercolors. Let the children cover the paper with upper- and lowercase *C's* to make a collage of the letter *C*.

# Phonics

## Cute Cakes

Give each child a photocopy of the cake pattern on page 68. Tell the children that they will be decorating cakes today. Ask them to write upper- and lowercase *C's* all over the top and sides of their cakes.

 *Variation:* Let the children help you make cupcakes. Let them use icing to write upper- and lowercase *C's* on top of their cupcakes before eating them.

## C Snack

Help the children brainstorm foods whose names begin with *C*, such as corn on the cob, cake, candy, cookies, carrots, cucumbers, cantaloupe, and coconut. Let the children plan the *C* foods they would like to eat for a *C* Snack.

## Cool Cat

Read the following rhyme to the children. As the children become familiar with the rhyme, let them fill in the rhyming *C* words at the end of each verse.

There's a very cool cat
Who's traveled near and far.
There's a very cool cat
Driving in a car.

There's a very cool cat
Sitting on your lap.
There's a very cool cat
Wearing a cool cap.

There's a very cool cat
Wearing a suit.
There's a very cool cat
Looking very cute.

There's a very cool cat
On the ocean in a boat.
There's a very cool cat
Wearing a cool coat.

## Phonics

# Dd

## Doodle D's

Give each child a *D*-shape cut out of construction paper. Talk about what it means to doodle. Then let the children use markers or crayons to doodle all over their letter *D* shapes. Hang the children's doodle *D's* around the room or on a bulletin board.

## Dig for D's

Collect an assortment of three-dimensional letter shapes, such as magnetic alphabet letters, wooden letters (available at craft stores), or alphabet puzzle pieces. Set out a selection of letters (about half of them should be *D's*). Fill a dishpan with dirt or dried beans. Hide the letters in the dishpan. Let the children take turns digging through the dirt or dried beans to find the letter *D's*.

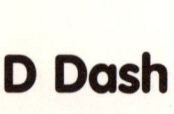

## D Dash

Write *D's* and other letters on index cards. Place the cards in a large indoor play area. Let the children dash around the room, picking up as many *D's* as they can find, but leaving the other letters where they are. When all of the *D's* have been found, have the children dash around the room to pick up all of the other letters.

 *Hint:* Instead of writing letters on index cards, use the alphabet card patterns on pages 74–80 to make the letter cards for this activity.

## Dough D's

Purchase enough refrigerator breadsticks for each child to have one. Have the children wash their hands. Give each child a piece of foil and one of the refrigerator breadsticks. Have them gently form their dough into the shape of an upper- or lowercase *D*. Use a toothpick to etch each child's name onto his or her piece of foil. Place the foil pieces on baking sheets. Bake the children's letters according to the package directions. When the letters are cool, let the children enjoy eating their dough *D's*. If you wish, let the children dunk their *D's* into dip.

## Daffodil D's

Set out construction paper and paper baking cups. Have each child select a sheet of construction paper and write two or three large lowercase *d's* on his or her paper. Each lowercase *d* will be the stem and leaf of a daffodil. Show the children how to flatten a paper baking cup and make cuts around the edges for petals. Have them glue a flattened baking cup to the top of each of their lowercase *d's*. Then help the children glue a whole baking cup to the center of each flattened cup to complete their flowers.

## Roll for D

Have the children sit in a circle. Let one child roll a die and say the number that comes up. Together, name that many *D* words. For example, if the child rolled a four, you would have to name four words that begin with the letter *D*, such as *day, deer, doll, duck*. Continue until each child has had a chance to roll the die. To make the game more challenging, try not to repeat any of the *D* words said before.

## Dance for D's

Have the children stand in a circle. Ask them to listen carefully as you say a variety of words, some beginning with the letter *D* and some not. Have the children dance around the circle whenever they hear a word that begins with the letter *D*.

## Ee

### Elbow E's

Give each child an *E*-shape cut out of construction paper. Set out elbow macaroni, small bowls of glue, and paintbrushes. Let the children brush their letter *E's* with glue, then have them arrange the elbow macaroni all over the paper. While the children are working, ask them to think about why this macaroni is called elbow macaroni. (Because the pieces of macaroni are bent like elbows.) Hang the children's elbow *E's* all around your room.

### Envelopes for E's

Give each child an envelope with an upper- and lowercase *E* written on it. Set out ready-to-be-recycled magazines and newspapers. Let your children look through the magazines and newspapers to find upper- and lowercase *E's*. Have them cut out the *E's* and place them in their envelopes.

### Enter with E's

For each child, write the letter *E* on an index card. Write other letters on a few more index cards. Place the cards on a table by your door. As the children arrive at school, explain to them that they can only enter if they have the letter *E*. Let them look through the cards on the table to find one with the letter *E*. Then let them enter the classroom with their *E's*.

 *Extension:* Do this each time your children must enter the classroom, such as after recess, after lunch, or after going to the library.

 *Hint:* Instead of writing letters on index cards, use the alphabet card patterns on pages 74–80 to make the letter cards for this activity.

## Edible E's

Let the children make *E's* they can eat. Give each child a plate with four pretzel sticks, four strips of cheese, four carrot sticks, and four short pieces of licorice on it. Show them how to arrange the four pretzel sticks into an uppercase *E*. Have them arrange their strips of cheese, carrot sticks, and licorice pieces into uppercase *E's*. Then let them eat their edible *E's*.

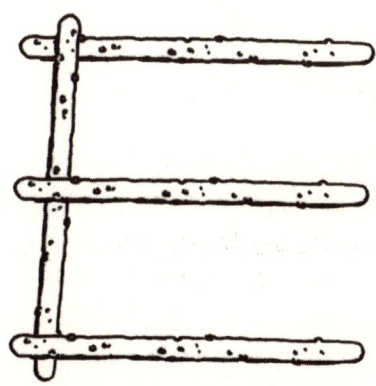

## E's on Eggs

Cut egg shapes out of construction paper. Cut a big basket shape out of brown paper and hang it on a wall or a bulletin board. Give each child one or more egg shapes. Let the children write upper- and lowercase *E's* on their eggs. Have them tape their eggs to the paper basket.

## Echo E's

Explain to the children that an echo is a sound that repeats. Tell them that you will say a word. If the word begins with the *E* sound, they should echo, or repeat, the word. If the word does not begin with the *E* sound, they should stay silent. Start with a few *E* words, such as *enter*, *elf*, and *egg*. Have the children echo each of these words. Then begin mixing in other words. Challenge the children to listen closely to each word and to only echo the *E* words.

## On the Net

On long strips of paper, write simple three-letter words with the short *e* in the medial position, such as *beg*, *let*, *get*, *jet*, *hen*, and *pen*. Write other simple words, such as *mat*, *dog*, *pin*, and *hug* on other long strips of paper. String a volleyball or badminton net between two chairs. Let the children find the words with the short *e* sound in them and weave them in and out of the net.

## Phonics

# Ff

## Feather F's

Give each child an *F*-shape cut out of construction paper. Let the children glue feathers all over their letters. Talk about the "fine, fancy, fabulous, feathers" they are gluing on their letters. When they are finished, hang their feather *F's* all around your room.

## Fan for F's

Show the children how to make a fan by folding a sheet of paper back and forth several times. Help each child make a fan. Write *F's* and other letters on index cards. Hold up the letter cards one at a time. Whenever they see a letter *F* card, have the children fan themselves with their folded fans.

*Hint:* Instead of writing letters on index cards, use the alphabet card patterns on pages 74–80 to make the letter cards for this activity.

## Follow the Footprints

Trace around your foot or one of the children's feet. Use this as a pattern to cut twenty foot shapes out of construction paper. Write upper- and lowercase *F's* on the foot shapes. Then use them to make a path for the children to follow.

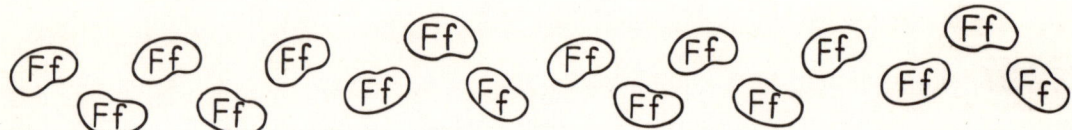

## Fish F's

Turn a bulletin board into a large aquarium by covering it with blue butcher paper. Add details such as sea grass and rocks. Give each child a photocopy of the fish pattern on page 69. Let the children use crayons or markers to decorate their fish shapes with upper- and lowercase *F's*. Then have the children cut out their fish shapes and attach them to your aquarium.

## Foamy F's

Have the children put on aprons and roll up their sleeves for this activity. Spray small mounds of shaving cream foam onto a table and let the children spread it around with their fingers and hands. Then have the children use their fingers to write upper- and lowercase *F's* in the foam.

## Fact or Fiction

Explain to the children that when you say something that is true, you are stating a fact, and when you say something that is not true, it is called fiction. Let each child make a statement about an object whose name begins with the letter *F*. Have the other children say whether the statement is fact (true) or fiction (false). For example, a child could say, "The fence is purple," and everyone would say, "Fiction." Or, a child could say, "Fish live in water," and everyone would reply, "Fact."

## Fiddle Dee

Recite the following rhyme with the children. Have them listen carefully to the made-up word at the end of the second line in each verse, then let them fill in the rhyming word that begins with the letter *F* on the last line.

Fiddle dee, fiddle dee,
Fiddle dee "dence."
Will you fiddle on my fence?

Fiddle dee, fiddle dee,
Fiddle dee "dield."
Will you fiddle in my field?

Fiddle dee, fiddle dee,
Fiddle dee "darm."
Will you fiddle on my farm?

Fiddle dee, fiddle dee,
Fiddle dee "dox."
Will you fiddle with my fox?

## Phonics

# Gg

## Gift G's

Give each child a *G*-shape cut out of construction paper. Cut small squares out of gift wrap. Let the children glue the squares of gift wrap all over their letter *G* shapes. Hang the children's gift *G*'s all around your room.

## G Game

Divide twelve index cards into six pairs. On the first pair, use a red marker to write an uppercase *G* on one of the cards and a lowercase *G* on the other. Repeat for each pair of cards, using a different color each time. Mix up the cards and arrange them face up on a table. Let the children find the *G's* in the matching colors.

## Give Me a G

Make alphabet letter cards using the patterns on pages 74–80. Make photocopies of the *G* alphabet card (enough for half of your class) and photocopies of several other alphabet cards (enough for the other half of your class). Pass out the alphabet cards. Ask the children to look at their cards. Say *Give me a G*, and have the children holding *G* alphabet cards come up and give you their cards. Then have the children holding other letters give you their cards. Mix up the alphabet cards and pass them out again.

 *Hint:* Make additional photocopies of the alphabet letter cards so that all the children can be given a *G* alphabet card and an alphabet card for another letter. Have each child come up one at a time to give you just his or her *G* card.

## Guess the G's

Describe an object whose name begins with *G*. Have the children guess what it is. Make sure that all of their guesses are words that begin with the *G* sound. If necessary, set out pictures of *G* objects for the children to look at while they are guessing.

## Glitter G's

Cut large *G*-shapes out of heavy paper. Let the children paint their letters green. Have them sprinkle green glitter all over the wet paint. Then help them shake off the excess glitter.

 *Variation:* Have the children brush glue all over their *G*-shapes. Then let them sprinkle on gold glitter.

## Get Through the Gate

Set up a gate in your room. This could be a ribbon strung between two chairs, a cardboard tube resting across two tables, or two chairs pushed together. Set out index cards and pencils. Explain to the children that in order to get through the gate, they must write an upper- or lowercase *G* (or both) on an index card and hand it to you, the gatekeeper. Then let them get through the gate.

## Go for G

Sing the following song with the children. After they are familiar with the song, let them think of other *G* words to substitute for *game, goat, gift, good, goldfish, and gallop*.

Sung to: "Three Blind Mice"

Go for G.
Go for G.
I go for G.
I go for G.
Game, goat, gift, and good, you see.
I really go for the words of *G.*
Goldfish and gallop sound golden to me.
I go for *G.*

## Hh

### Heart H's

Give each child an *H*-shape cut out of construction paper. Let them cover their *H's* with all kinds of hearts, such as sticker hearts, paper hearts, and prints from heart-shaped rubber stamps. Or, show them how to use a small heart stencil to draw hearts all over their *H's*. When the children are finished, hang their heart *H's* all around your room.

### Hello to H

Write *H's* and other letters on index cards. Hold up the letter cards one at a time. Whenever the children see the letter *H*, have them say "Hello, H!"

*Hint:* Instead of writing letters on index cards, use the alphabet card patterns on pages 74–80 to make the letter cards for this activity.

### Hammer H's

Find a handful of golf tees. Use a permanent marker to write an upper- or lowercase *H* on half of the golf tees and other alphabet letters on the other half. Put the golf tees in a box. Find an old plastic-foam cooler. Turn the cooler upside down. Set out the golf tees along with a child-size hammer. Let the children take turns hammering only the *H* golf tees into the cooler.

## Easy H's

Give each child six craft sticks. Show the children how to arrange three craft sticks to make an uppercase *H*. Let each child use his or her craft sticks to make two uppercase *H's* and glue them to a sheet of heavy paper.

## A Hoop of H's

Hang a large plastic hoop from the ceiling. Collect several index cards (or squares of paper) for each child. Set out the cards, markers or crayons, and small pieces of tape. Let the children use the markers or crayons to write upper- and lowercase *H's* on the cards. Then have them tape their *H* cards all around the hoop.

## Hunt for H Sounds

In your room, count how many objects you have whose names begin with *H*. Look for objects, such as a *hammer*, a *house* for a doll, a *horse*, a *helmet*, a *hat*, a *heart*, and a *horn*. If you do not have many objects, add a few for this activity. Place a large plastic hoop in the middle of your floor. Have the children hunt around the room for objects whose names start with the letter *H*. Each time they find one, have them place the object in the hoop.

## If You Like H

Sing the following song with the children. Have them act out the motions as described in the song. Let them think of other *H* words to substitute for horse and hoop.

Sung to: "If You're Happy and You Know It"

If you like *H* a lot, raise your hand.
If you like *H* a lot, raise your hand.
If you like *H* a lot,
Horse and hoop must hit the spot.
If you like *H* a lot, raise your hand.

## Phonics

# Ii

## Invisible I's

Cut an I-shape out of white construction paper for each child. Use a white crayon to write upper- and lowercase I's on each child's letter. Be sure to press down hard. Give each child one of the letters. Let the children brush watercolors over their letter I's to make the invisible I's appear. When all of the I's are showing, hang the children's letters around the room.

## Insect I's

Use the alphabet letter card patterns on pages 74–80 for this activity. Make photocopies of the I alphabet card (enough for half of the children) and photocopies of several other letters (enough for the other half of the children). Mix up the cards and pass them out. Have the children look at their cards. If they have one of the letter I cards, have them pretend to be insects and fly all around the room. If they have one of the other cards, have them sit down. Mix up the cards and play the game again.

## I's for the Igloo

Write I's and other letters on index cards. Turn a shoebox into an igloo by covering it with white paper. Draw a picture of an igloo on one side. Then, cut a hole in the side of the box and have the children take turns sorting through the alphabet cards and pushing the I cards through the hole and into the igloo.

 *Hint:* Instead of writing letters on index cards, use the alphabet card patterns on pages 74–80 to make the letter cards for this activity.

Published by Totline Publications. Copyright protected.

# Inside I's

Give each child a sheet of plain paper with a 5-inch box drawn in the middle of it. Set out markers, crayons, or pencils. Have the children look at their papers. Ask them to point to the inside of the box on their papers. Then have each child write upper- and lowercase *I's* inside the box on his or her paper.

# Invent an I

Set out a variety of decorating materials, such as chenille stems, sequins, ribbons, poms, fabric scraps, craft sticks, and glitter glue. Let the children use the materials to create as many different kinds of *I's* as they can. Help them glue their *I's* to a length of butcher paper. Hang their inventive *I's* on a wall or a bulletin board.

# I Is for Instruments

Give each child an instrument. (Rhythm instruments work well for this. Make instruments from pots and pans and wooden spoons if necessary.) Have them listen as you say words one a time, some beginning with the letter *I*, some beginning with other letters. Have the children play their instruments each time you say a word that begins with *I*.

# Rhymes With It

Play this game to introduce the short *i* sound in the middle of a word. Encourage the children to listen for the *it* sound as you say some simple three-letter words. If the word you say rhymes with *it* (*bit, hit, pit, bit, fit,* etc.), have the children sit down. If the word you say does not rhyme with *it* (*cat, bet, dig, lot, bug*), have the children stand up. (If the children are already sitting, they stay sitting. If the children are already standing, they stay standing.) Repeat as many times as you wish.

## Phonics

# Jj

## Jeweled J's

Collect a variety of colors and sizes of sequin jewels. Give each child a J-shape cut out of construction paper. Let the children glue the jewels all over their letter J shapes. When the children are finished, hang their jeweled J's all around your room.

## Jar of J's

Find a large jar. (A food service jar for mayonnaise works well.) Label the jar with a letter J. Collect about twenty clothespins. Write an upper- or lowercase J on half of the clothespins. Write a different letter on the remaining half. Let the children take turns standing beside the jar and dropping only the J clothespins into it.

## Jack-in-the-Box

Write J's and other letters on index cards. Have the children crouch down close to the floor. Hold up the letter cards one at a time. Each time they see the letter J, have the children jump up like jack-in-the-boxes.

*Hint:* Instead of writing letters on index cards, use the alphabet card patterns on pages 74–80 to make the letter cards for this activity.

## Jellybean J's

Give each child a paper plate and a handful of jellybeans. Show the children how to arrange the jellybeans on their plates to make upper- and lowercase J's. Do they have enough jellybeans to make a J of all one color? Can they arrange the jellybeans in a color pattern while making their letter J's? Let the children eat their jellybeans once they have arranged them on their plates.

Published by Totline Publications. Copyright protected.     1-57029-470-4  1•2•3 Phonics

Phonics

## J Journal

Make a journal for each child by stapling five sheets of paper together. Help the children write "My *Jj* Journal" on the front of their stapled papers. Have the children write upper- and lowercase *J's* on the pages of their journals. Make a list of words that start with *J* for the children to copy into their journals. Try short, easy words, such as *jet, jar, job,* and *jam*.

 *Extension:* If you wish, let the children look through magazines to find pictures of objects whose names begin with *J*. Let them glue the *J* pictures into their *J* journals.

## J Snack

Have the children help you plan a *J* snack. Let them vote on their favorite juice. Have them choose two or three varieties of jam or jelly to sample. Set out the juice and toast, along with the jam or jelly. Let the children spread the jam or jelly of their choice on their toast.

 *Extension:* Have each child say a word that begins with a *J* before being dismissed to snack.

## Jolly, Jolly J

Sing the following song with the children. As they become familiar with it, let them think of *J* words to substitute for *jeans, jog, jam,* and *jeep*.

Sung to: "The Farmer in the Dell"

    Oh, jolly, jolly *J*,
    Oh, jolly, jolly *J*,
    Jeans and jog
    And jam and jeep
    All begin with *J*.

## Phonics

# Kk

## Kernel K's

Give each child a *K*-shape cut out of construction paper. Set out a bowl of popcorn kernels, several small bowls of glue, and paintbrushes. Let the children brush glue all over their letter *K's*. Then have them arrange popcorn kernels on the glue. Encourage them to cover as much of their *K* shapes as they can. When the glue is dry, hang the children's kernel *K's* all around your room.

## Keep the K's

Use the alphabet card patterns on pages 74–80. Make ten photocopies of the *K* alphabet card and ten photocopies of other alphabet cards. Mix up the cards and place them in a pile facedown. Invite one of the children to join you. Have the child turn over the first alphabet card. If it is one of the letter *K* cards, have the child keep the card. If it is not, have the child give the card to you. Repeat with the remaining cards, until the child has kept all of the *K* cards.

## Kettle of K's

Collect the alphabet cards from the "Keep the K's" activity on this page. Find a small kettle that the children will be able to hold and pass around easily. Have the children sit in a circle. Mix up the alphabet cards and pass one out to each of the children. Give the kettle to one of the children. Have the child look at his or her alphabet card. If it is a *K* card, have the child put the card in the kettle and pass the kettle to the next child. If it is not a *K* card, have the child keep his or her card and pass on the kettle. When the kettle has been passed all around the circle, take out the cards to make sure only the K cards were put in it. Collect all of the cards, mix them up, and play the game again.

# Phonics

## K Kites

Give each child a photocopy of the kite pattern on page 70. Let the children use markers or crayons to write upper- and lowercase *K's* all over their kite shapes. When the kite shapes are completely decorated with *K's*, have the children cut them out. Help them add yarn tails and paper bow shapes to complete their kites. Hang the children's *K* kites high up on a wall or from the ceiling.

## Keyed-Up K's

Tape several old keys to a table top. Show the children how to place a sheet of paper over the keys and rub over the paper with an unwrapped crayon to make key rubbings. Have the children write an upper- and lowercase *K* by each key rubbing.

## K's for the King

Make a paper crown and write upper- and lowercase *K's* all over it. Ask one child to be the king. Give him or her the crown to wear. Let the other children take turns bringing imaginary gifts to the king. Make sure each gift's name begins with the letter *K*. Sing the following song as the children play this game. Let the child name his or her gift as indicated in the song.

Sung to: "The Muffin Man"

Do you have a gift for the king
A gift for the king, a gift for the king?
Do you have a gift for the king?
Yes, I have a _____.

 *Variation:* Instead of bringing imaginary gifts to the king, use real objects or pictures of objects whose names begin with *K*.

## Kick a K

In a large, open area, have the children stand in a circle. Gently kick a ball to one of the children. Have that child say a word that begins with the letter *K*. Then have him or her kick the ball to another child before sitting in an area away from the circle. Let the children take turns naming a *K* word and kicking the ball until everyone is sitting down. Then play the game again.

## Phonics

# Ll

## Lacy L's

Collect lace of all kinds and colors. Give each child an *L*-shape cut out of construction paper. Set out the lace, scissors, and glue. Let the children cut the lace into small pieces to glue onto their letter shapes. When their lacy *L's* are finished, hang them all around your room.

## Light Up the L's

Cut *L*-shapes and other letter shapes out of construction paper. Attach the alphabet letters to a wall. Give several children flashlights. Turn off the room lights and have the children with flashlights only shine their lights on the letter *L's* on the wall.

## L Laundry

Use the clothing patterns on page 71 as guides for cutting clothing shapes out of construction paper. Write an upper- or lowercase *L* on most of the clothing shapes and other letters on the remaining shapes. Put the clothing "laundry" in a small laundry basket. String a clothesline between two chairs. Let the children take turns sorting the laundry and hanging up only the *L* laundry on the clothesline.

## Label L's

Give each child a sheet of plain labels. (Sheets of labels can be found at office supply stores.) Let the children write upper- and lowercase *L's* on their labels. Then have them stick their *L* labels onto sheets of construction paper.

*Variation:* Purchase labels that are removable. Have the children write upper- and lowercase *L's* on the labels. Then let the children place the *L* labels on objects whose names begin with *L*.

# Lavender Lists

Cut sheets of lavender construction paper lengthwise into thirds to make paper for lists. Let the children use lavender markers or crayons to write upper- and lowercase *L*'s on their lavender lists. Or make a list of words that begin with *L* for the children to copy onto their lists.

# Lullaby

Sing this lullaby with the children. Pretend to rock a baby to sleep while you sing. At the end of the song, have the children notice that every word begins with the letter *L*.

Sung to: "Twinkle, Twinkle, Little Star"

> La, la, la, la, lullaby,
> Lovely little lullaby.
> Little lambs love lullabies.
> Ladybugs love lullabies.
> La, la, la, la, lullaby,
> Lovely little lullaby.

# Lion L's

Have the children pretend to be lions. Let them practice their lion roar. Then ask them to listen carefully while you say several words. Each time they hear a word that begins with the letter *L*, have them roar like lions.

## Phonics

# Mm

## Musical M's

Give each child an *M*-shape cut out of construction paper and a few markers. Play some music. Ask the children to let the music inspire them as they decorate their letters. If the music is soft and gentle, encourage them to make soft and gentle lines and swirls. If the music is loud and jumpy, have them make jumpy points and zigzags. Play several different types of music while the children work. When they are finished, hang the children's musical *M's* all around your room.

## M Mats

Arrange carpet squares all around your room. Using masking tape, "write" the letter *M* on two-thirds of the mats and other letters on the remaining mats. Play some music and have the children march around the room. When the music stops, have each child find an *M* mat to stand on or touch. Some *M* mats will have more than one child at them. Play the music once more and let the children march around the room again.

## Mailing M's

Write *M's* and other letters on index cards. Cover a shoebox with construction paper and decorate it to look like a mailbox. Be sure to cover the lid separately. Cut a slit in the lid and write an upper- and lowercase *M* beside it. Let the children take turns mailing only the *M* alphabet cards in the *M* mailbox.

 *Hint:* Instead of writing letters on index cards, use the alphabet card patterns on pages 74–80 to make the letter cards for this activity.

## M Mountain

Cover a table with butcher paper. Use a black marker to draw a large mountain on the butcher paper. Let the children use crayons or markers to write upper- and lowercase *M*'s all over the *M* mountain.

## M's in the Middle

On a sheet of plain paper, write *M* ___ *M* and *m* ___ *m* several times. Make a photocopy of the paper for each child. Give the children the papers and pencils. Point out the upper- and lowercase *M*'s on their papers, as well as the space in between them. Ask the children to write upper- and lowercase *M*'s in the middle of the *M*'s on their papers.

## M Is for Music Box

Show the children a music box. Demonstrate how to gently wind up the music box to make it play. Let one of the children wind up the box. While the music is playing, ask the children to name as many words as they can think of that start with the letter *M*. Write the words on a sheet of chart paper. When the music box stops, read back all the *M* words they named.

## Measuring M

Let the children use measuring sticks (rulers) to measure objects whose names begin with *M*, such as a mitten, a mirror, or a map. As the children work, repeat this rhyme, substituting the names of the objects they are measuring for *mitten* and the lengths for *6 inches*.

> Measuring the mitten,
> I'll show you how.
> Measuring the mitten,
> It's 6 inches now.

## Phonics

# Nn

## Number N's

Give each child an *N*-shape cut out of construction paper. Let the children use crayons or markers to write numbers all over their letters. Or, if you prefer, let the children cover their letters with number stickers (available at school and office supply stores). When the children finish, hang their number *N's* all around your room.

## Do You Need an N?

Write *N's* and other letters on index cards. Mix up the cards. Have the children sit in a circle. Give each child one of the alphabet cards. Ask each child, *Do you need an N?* If the child already has an *N* card have him or her say, *No, I do not need an N.* If the child does not have an *N* alphabet card, have the child nod his or her head and say, *I need an N.* Give each child who nods his or her head an *N* alphabet card. Then collect the cards and play the game again.

 *Hint:* Instead of writing letters on index cards, use the alphabet card patterns on pages 74–80 to make the letter cards for this activity.

## Nest of N's

Make a pretend bird's nest out of a large grocery bag. Roll the sides of the grocery bag down several times. Fill the bag with brown paper grass or raffia (available at craft stores). Collect a dozen plastic eggs. Use a permanent marker to write the letter *N* on half of the eggs and other letters on the remaining eggs. Place the bird's nest and the eggs on a table. Let the children take turns putting the *N* eggs in the nest.

## Nickel N's

Write an upper- and lowercase *N* on a large sheet of construction paper. Set out the paper and a container of nickels. Let the children take turns arranging the nickels on the outlines of the upper- and lowercase *N's*.

## N's at Night

Give each child a sheet of midnight blue construction paper and a piece of chalkboard chalk. Let the children pretend their papers are the night sky. Have them write upper- and lowercase *N's* all over their night sky. Let them add other details to their night sky pictures, such as stars and the moon.

## Noodle Necklaces

Purchase several varieties of noodles suitable for stringing, such as macaroni, rigatoni, and wagon wheels. Let the children lace the noodles onto lengths of yarn to make noodle necklaces.

 *Extension:* Write upper- and lowercase *N's* on 2-inch squares of paper. Punch a hole in the top of each square. Let the children string letter *N's* onto their noodle necklaces.

## What Do You Notice?

Have the children look around the room to notice and name objects whose names begin with *N*. Write down all of the objects they find. Sing the following song with the children, substituting the name of something they found for *necklace*.

Sung to: "The Muffin Man"

Notice and name the *N's* with me,
The *N's* with me, the *N's* me.
Notice and name the *N's* with me.
The first *N* is a necklace.

## Phonics

# Oo

### Polka-Dot O's

Give each child an *O*-shape cut out of construction paper. Then set out crayons, markers, and *o*-shaped stickers and let the children decorate their *O's* with polka dots. Hang the polka-dot *O's* all around your room.

### O's Go On

Write *O's* and other letters on index cards. Set out the alphabet cards and an oval shape cut out of construction paper. Let the children take turns sorting the alphabet cards and placing the *O* letter cards on the oval shape. Then have them take the *O* cards off of the oval and play the game again.

 *Hint:* Instead of writing letters on index cards, use the alphabet card patterns on pages 74–80 to make the letter cards for this activity.

### How Many O's?

Challenge the children to think of as many different ways as they can to make the letter *O* with their bodies. Can they make an *O* with their fingers? With their hands? With their arms? With their whole body? Can they work together to make an even bigger letter *O*?

## That's Odd

Have the children sit in a circle. Ask them to listen carefully as you say a word. If the word begins with the letter *O*, have them make an *O* with their fingers. If the word does not begin with the letter *O*, have them say, *That's odd.* Let the children take turns naming words that do and do not begin with the letter *O*.

## In the Box

Write an *O* on the outside of a box. On index cards, write three-letter words that have the short *o* sound in the middle. Use words, such as *box, fox, dog, fog, jot* and *cot*. On other index cards, write three-letter words that do not have the short *o* sound in the middle, such as *cab, set, dig*, and *rug*. Have the children sit in a circle and place the *O* box in the center of the circle. Give each child a word card. One at a time, have each child stand up to share his or her word card. Help the child read the card, if necessary. Put words with the short *o* sound in the box. Place words with other letter sounds on the floor beside the box. When each child has had a turn, mix up the cards and pass them out again.

## O Octopus

Show the children how to turn the letter *O* into an octopus. Have each child draw an *O* in the middle of a sheet of construction paper and then draw eight octopus arms coming out from the *O*. Let the children add facial features inside the *O*, if they wish. Let the children make as many *O* octopi on their papers as they would like.

### Phonics

# Pp

## Purple P's

Give each child a *P*-shape cut out of construction paper. Cover a table with newspaper. Set out purple paint and paintbrushes. Let the children paint their letters purple. If you wish, have purple glitter available for them to sprinkle on the paint while it is still wet. When the letters are dry, hang the children's purple *P*'s all around your room.

## Penny Pitch

Write upper- and lowercase *P*'s on each of several paper plates. Write other letters on a few more plates. Place the plates on the floor. Let the children take turns pitching pennies only onto the *P* plates.

## Puzzle Partners

Photocopy the *P* alphabet card on page 77 so that you have one card for every two children in your class. Cut out the letter *P* cards. Cut each *P* card into two puzzle pieces, being sure to make each puzzle piece a different shape. Pass out the puzzle pieces to the children. Have the children find their puzzle partners to complete their *P* alphabet cards.

## P Pancakes

Mix up a batch of pancake batter with the children. Working with one child, let the child watch as you carefully pour pancake batter on a hot griddle, making the letter *P*. (Be sure to use caution when working with electrical appliances around young children.) Have the child notice that when you flip the pancake over, the *P* is backwards. Place the pancake *P* on the child's plate so it reads correctly. Let the children eat their pancakes with butter and syrup. Or help them spread peanut butter on their *P* pancakes.

# Parade of Pink and Purple P's

Hang a length of butcher paper on a wall at the children's eye level. Draw three horizontal lines across the middle of the paper. Place a table near the butcher paper. Arrange pink and purple crayons, markers, pencil, paint, and chalk on the table. Let the children use the writing utensils to write pink and purple *P's* on the lines, making a parade of *P's*.

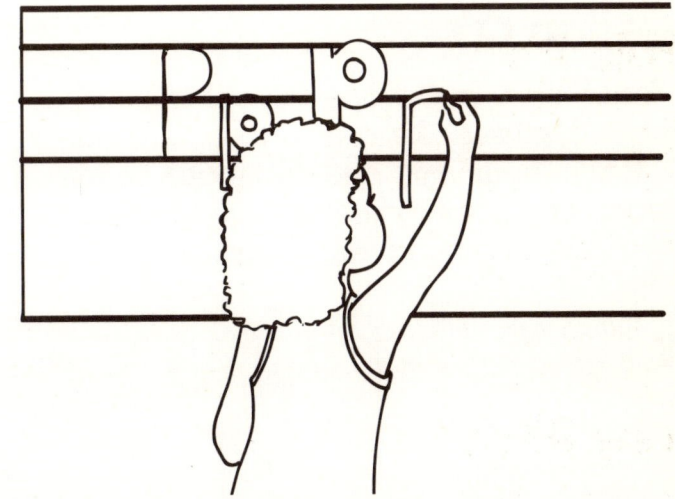

# Pass the Puppet

Have the children sit in a circle. Recite the following rhyme while you pass a puppet around. At the end of the rhyme, have the child holding the puppet say a word that begins with *P*.

Pass the puppet
Around and around.
Pass the puppet
Without a sound.
Pass the puppet
So carefully.
Now name a word
That begins with *P*.

# Pool Party

Collect an assortment of stuffed animals or pictures of animals whose names begin with *P*. For example, you could have a *pig*, a *panda*, a *panther*, a *parrot*, a *penguin*, a *python*, and a *puppy*. Add other stuffed animals or pictures of animals whose names do not begin with the letter *P*, such as a cat, a cow, a tiger, a frog, a bear, and a horse. Set out a child's wading pool and all of the animals. Tell the children that there is going to be a pool party for animals whose names begin with *P*. Let them find those animals and put them in the pool.

# Qq

## Question Q's

Give each child a *Q*-shape cut out of construction paper. Show the children how to write a question mark. Have them write question marks all over their *Q* shapes. When they are finished, hang their question *Q's* all around your room.

*Extension:* Talk about what a question mark means and when you use it.

## Quacking for Q's

Write *Q's* and other letters on index cards. Mix up the cards. Show the letter cards to the children one at a time. Have them quack whenever they see the letter *Q*.

*Hint:* Instead of writing letters on index cards, use the alphabet card patterns on pages 74–80 to make the letter cards for this activity.

## Quills for Q

Make your own quills by purchasing large feathers (available at craft stores) and sharpening the ends with a sharp knife. Set out the quills, small bowls of tempera paint, and paper. Show the children how to dip the end of a feather quill into the paint and then use it to write. Have them use the quills to write upper- and lowercase *Q's* all over sheets of paper.

*Variation:* Instead of sharpening the ends of feathers to make quills, make pretend quills by taping feathers to the ends of pencils. Let the children write with the pencil quills.

## Q Quilt

Cut construction paper into 9-inch squares. Give each child one of the paper squares. Have the children use markers or crayons to write upper- and lowercase *Q's* all over their squares. Encourage them to make as many *Q's* as they can. Arrange all of the children's squares together on a flat surface. Tape the squares together to make a *Q* quilt.

## Quest for Q's

Make twenty photocopies of the *Q* alphabet card pattern on page 78. Cut out the cards. Hide the cards around your room. Let the children go on a quest for the *Q* letter cards. Each time they find a *Q* card, have them put it into a quart jar with the letter *Q* written on it.

## Questions About Q

Ask the children the following questions. Remind them that the answer to each question is a word that begins with *Q*. Think of other questions to ask the children.

What do you use to keep warm? (*quilt*)
What is 25 cents? (*quarter*)
What is the opposite of loud? (*quiet*)
What is another word for hunt? (*quest*)
What kind of pen is made from a feather? (*quill*)
What am I asking? (*questions*)
What is another word for fast? (*quick*)

## Quickly, Quickly

Sing the following song with the children. Let them think of other *Q* words to substitute for *quilt, queen, quiet, quest,* and *quill.*

Sung to: "Frere Jacques"

Quickly, quickly,
Quickly, quickly,
Can you say?
Can you say?
Quilt and queen and quiet,
Quilt and queen and quiet,
Quest and quill,
Quest and quill.

# Rr

## Ruler R's

Give each child an *R*-shape cut out of construction paper. Show the children how to use a ruler and a pencil to draw a straight line. Let them use the rulers to draw "rules" (lines) all over their letter shapes. When they are finished, hang their ruler *R's* all around your room.

## R Race

Write upper- and lowercase *R's* on twenty index cards. Place all of the cards at one end of your room and a rug at the other end. Have the children stand by the rug. One at a time, have them "race-walk" to the cards, pick up an *R* letter card and race back to put the *R* card on the rug. When all of the *R* cards have been returned to the rug, the game is over. If you wish, let the children race the clock or divide into two teams and race against one another.

 *Variation:* Play this game outside and let the children run to collect the *R* letter cards.

 *Hint:* Instead of writing letters on index cards, use the *R* alphabet card pattern on page 78 to make the letter cards for this activity.

## R's for Rubbing

Cut several *R*-shapes out of cardboard. Cover each *R*-shape with a different textured material such as sandpaper, fabric, rice, or corrugated cardboard. Show the children how to place plain sheets of paper over the *R*-shapes and rub an unwrapped crayon over it to create an *R* rubbing.

# Phonics

## Robot R's

Help each child use a black marker to write a large *R* on a plain sheet of paper. Then let the children use crayons, straws, chenille stems, and other items to add details to the letter *R's*, turning them into robots. For example, a child could add feet to the bottom of the *R*, antennae to the top, arms coming out of the sides, and a face in the round part.

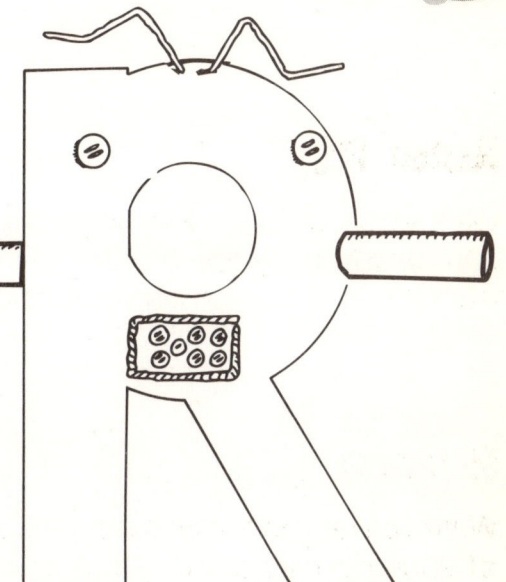

## Railroad Signs

Show the children a picture of a railroad crossing sign. Have them notice the two letters on the sign. Have the children make their own railroad crossing signs to hang around the room. Then let them pretend to be trains chugging around the room, tooting their horns whenever they chug past a railroad crossing sign.

## Room for R's

Section off a corner of your room. Explain to the children that this is your room for *R's*. Throughout the day, have the children look for objects whose names begin with *R*. Whenever they find one, have them put the object in the room for *R's*. At the end of the day, look at all the objects they have collected. Say the names of the objects together.

## Rocky Road Ice Cream

Serve up a dish of rocky road ice cream for each child. Have the children say words that begin with *R* before each bite.

## Sandy S's

Give each child an *S*-shape cut out of construction paper. Set out small bowls of glue and paintbrushes. Let the children brush glue all over their *S*-shapes. Then have them hold their letters over a box and sprinkle sand all over the glue. When the glue is dry, hang the children's sandy *S's* all around your room.

## Sack of S's

Find all different kinds of *S's* to hide in your room. Try alphabet blocks with the letter *S* on them, *S's* from a set of magnetic letters, *S's* cut out of ads and glued to index cards, wooden *S's* from craft stores, and others. Give each child a sack with the letter *S* written on it. Have the children find as many letter *S's* as they can to put in their sacks.

 *Variation:* Instead of using a variety of *S's*, make *S* letter cards by making photocopies of the *S* alphabet card pattern on page 78. Cut out the cards.

## On the S Side

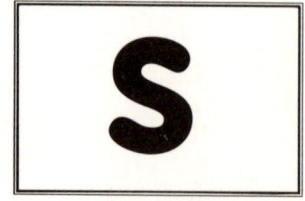

Write *S's* and other letters on index cards. Write the letter *S* on a sheet of construction paper and hang it up on one side of your room. Give each child one of the alphabet cards. Have the children look at their cards. If it is an *S* card, have them stand on the *S* side of the room. If it is not, have them stand on the other side. Collect the cards, mix them up, and play the game again.

 *Hint:* Instead of writing letters on index cards, use the alphabet card patterns on pages 74–80 to make the letter cards for this activity.

## Super S Supper

Help the children make a list of foods whose names begin with *S,* such as *sandwiches, salad, soup, sunflower seeds, sesame sticks, salsa, syrup, soy sauce,* and *salami.* Let them choose six or seven items to serve at a super *S* supper.

# S Surprises

Collect a variety of small surprises (party favors, small toys, treats, etc.) and place them in a suitcase. Show the suitcase to the children and tell them that it is filled with *S* surprises for them. However, explain that the suitcase only opens for the letter *S*. Set out paper and pencils. Let the children write six or seven *S's* on their papers. As the children finish, have them show their *S's* to the suitcase. Open up the suitcase and let the children choose their surprises.

*Variation:* If you wish, make the surprise something whose name begins with *S*, such as *suckers*.

# Sea of S's

Hang a length of butcher paper on a wall at the children's eye level. Draw a curvy line across the paper to represent the sea. Have the children use blue markers or crayons to write *S's* in the sea. Then make a photocopy of the sailboat pattern on page 72 for each child. Have the children cut out their sailboats, then have them write upper- and lowercase *S's* on the sails. Let them glue their sailboats on top of their sea of *S's*.

# Sing a Song

Sing the following song with the children. Let them think of other adjectives that begin with *S* to substitute for *super, silly, sad* and *serious*.

Sung to: "Skip to My Lou"

Sing, sing, sing a song,
Sing, sing, sing a song,
Sing, sing, sing a song.
Sing a song for *S*.

It's a super, silly song,
It's a super, silly song,
It's a super, silly song.
Sing a song for *S*.

It's a sad and serious song,
It's a sad and serious song,
It's a sad and serious song.
Sing a song for *S*.

# Phonics

## Tt

### Torn Tissue T's

Give each child a *T*-shape cut out of construction paper. Help the children tear colorful sheets of tissue paper into small pieces. Set out small bowls of glue and paintbrushes. Have them brush glue all over their letter *T*-shapes and then arrange the torn tissue on the glue. When the glue is dry, hang the children's torn tissue *T's* all around your room.

### Tic-Tac-Toe

Teach the children how to play tic-tac-toe. However, instead of using *X's* and *O's*, have the children use upper- and lowercase *T's* to mark their squares. Let them play as many games as they would like.

### T Team

Collect a dozen or more stuffed animals. Put a plain, removable label on each stuffed animal. Write the letter *T* on half of the labels and other letters on the remaining labels. Mix up the stuffed animals. Have the children find the stuffed animals with the letter *T* on them. This is the *T* team. Let the children line up the *T* team animals in the shape of the letter *T*.

### Tape T's

Give each child a sheet of construction paper. Tear off strips of masking tape and place them around the edge of the table. Let the children use the strips of masking tape to make upper- and lowercase *T's* on their construction paper.

# Phonics

## Tall T's

Cover part of a wall with butcher paper. Make sure the butcher paper reaches above the children's heads. Let the children use crayons or markers to reach up as high as they can to draw really tall upper- and lowercase *T's* on the paper.

 *Variation:* Take the children outside and let them use chalk to write tall upper- and lowercase *T's* on the sidewalk.

## Toss It

Set out a baby bathtub in the middle of the room. Set out several objects you can toss, whose names begin with *T*, such as a *towel*, a *teddy* bear, a *toothbrush*, a *tube* (cardboard), a *teaspoon*, and a *teabag*, plus a variety of objects that you can toss, whose names do not begin with *T*. Choose one child to begin. Have the child pick up one of the *T* objects and gently toss it in the tub while you sing the following song. Substitute the name of the object the child tossed in for *towel*.

Sung to: "The Farmer in the Dell"

> Toss it in the tub,
> Toss it in the tub
> It's your turn to toss in the towel.
> Toss it in the tub.

## Terrible or Terrific Tales

Explain to the children that *tale* is another word for *story*. Tell them a tale of your own. Try to use words that begin with *T* in your story. Make your story terrific (happy) or terrible (sad). At the end of your tale, have the children say, *How terrific!* if it was a happy story or *How terrible!* if it was a sad story. Then let the children take turns telling their own terrific or terrible tales.

## Phonics

# Uu

## Umpire U's

Give each child a *U*-shape cut out of white construction paper. Show the children a picture of an umpire dressed in a black and white shirt. Let the children use black crayons or markers to add black stripes to the white *U* letter shapes. Display the children's umpire *U's* all around your room.

## Usher in U's

Cut ticket shapes out of construction paper. Write the letter *U* on half of the tickets. Write other letters on the remaining tickets. Explain to the children that they must have a *U* ticket in order to be ushered to their seats. As each child finds a *U* ticket, usher the child to his or her seat. If you wish, let the children take turns being the usher.

## Up for U's

Write *U's* and other letters on index cards. Mix up the cards. Have the children sit in a circle. Show them the letter cards one at a time. If a card has the letter *U* on it, have the children stand up. If it is another letter, have them stay seated.

 *Hint:* Instead of writing letters on index cards, use the alphabet card patterns on pages 74–80 to make the letter cards for this activity.

## U's Underneath

Tape a length of butcher paper to the underside of a table. Let the children crawl under the table and write upper- and lowercase *U's* on the paper. Talk about how it feels to write when you are upside down.

# Umbrella U's

Give each child a photocopy of the umbrella pattern on page 73. Point out the space under the umbrella. Have the children use markers or crayons to write upper- and lowercase *U's* under the umbrella.

# U Song

Hold up an umbrella and invite one child to stand under it. Sing the following song. Let the child name three *U* words to substitute for *uncle, unless,* and *upset.* Have another child stand under the umbrella and sing the song again.

Sung to: "Frere Jacques"

Under the umbrella,
Under the umbrella,
You can say,
You can say
Uncle, unless, upset,
Uncle, unless, upset,
Under the umbrella,
Under the umbrella.

 *Variation:* Instead of saying words that begin with the letter *U,* let the children name words that have the short *u* medial sound.

# Short U Collages

Have the children help you think of words with the short *u* sound in the middle. Make a list of the words, such as *sun, hut, nut, cup, cub, mug, bug,* and *bun.* Let the children look through magazines to find pictures of these objects. Have the children cut out the pictures and glue them to sheets of construction paper to make short *u* collages. Or let them draw simple pictures of these objects. When they are finished, have them say the names of the objects in their collages.

## Phonics

# Vv

## Vivid V's

Give each child a V-shape cut out of construction paper. Set out markers in bright, vivid colors. Have the children decorate their letter V-shapes with the markers, making their letters as brightly colored as they can. When they are finished, hang their vivid V's all around your room.

## Visiting V's

Set out visitor name tags. Write an upper- and lowercase V on most of the tags. Write other upper- and lowercase letters on the other badges. Pretend that all of the children are visitors to your class today. Explain to your visitors that they must find and put on their V visitor badges.

## Veer Toward V

Draw a V-shaped path on a large sheet of construction paper. Let the children take turns driving toy cars up and down the V. Or, use chalk to draw a large V-shape on the sidewalk. Let the children drive child-size vehicles (tricycles, scooters, etc.) on the V path.

## V Volcanoes

Show your children how to turn the letter *V* into a volcano. Give each child a plain sheet of paper and a red and a brown crayon. Have the children use their brown crayons to draw two large upside-down *V's* at the tops of their papers to make the crater of the volcano. Have them continue using their brown crayons to add the sides to the volcanoes. Then let them use their red crayons to draw lines of lava shooting out
of their volcanoes. Let the children make as many *V* volcanoes as they would like.

## Viewing V's

Divide the children into groups of four. Ask two children from each group to lie on the floor to make the letter *V* with their bodies. Have the other children view their group's *V*. Let the children change places. Then divide the children into two large groups. Have one group work together to form a giant letter *V* while the other group views their work. Then have them switch positions.

## V Village

Tape a length of butcher paper to a table. Let the children use markers or cutout magazine pictures create a mural of a *V* village. Everything in the village should begin with the letter *v*, such as *villas*, *vehicles*, *volcanoes*, *vines*, *vans*, *vegetables*, *veterinarians*, *violets*, *vacuum* cleaners, and *visitors*.

## Ww

### Wavy W's

Give each child a *W*-shape cut out of construction paper. Show the children how to draw wavy lines. Let them use crayons or markers to make wavy lines all over their *W* letter shapes. When they are finished, hang their wavy *W's* all around your room.

### Wink and Wave for W

Write *W's* and other letters on index cards. Mix up the cards. Show the children how to wink with one eye. Let them practice winking. Then hold up the letter cards one at a time. Whenever they see a *W* card, have the children wink and wave at you.

 *Hint:* Instead of writing letters on index cards, use the alphabet card patterns on pages 74–80 to make the letter cards for this activity.

### Welcome W's

Write *W's* on index cards and hide them around your room. As the children arrive, explain that they are welcome to join you at circle time after they have found a card with a *W* written on it. Welcome the children individually as they show you their *W* cards and sit down at the circle.

# Walls of W's

Hang a length of butcher paper on the wall. Let the children use markers and crayons to write upper- and lowercase *W's* all over the paper-covered wall. (Remind the children that real walls are not for writing on.)

*Variation:* Instead of walls, let the children use tempera paint to write upper- and lowercase *W's* on windows. (Add a few drops of liquid soap to the tempera paint to make it easier to wash off.)

# Wire W's

Purchase colorful bead wire and cut it into 6-inch lengths. (Bead wire is available at craft stores.) Give each child several pieces of the wire. Show the children how to bend their wires to make *W's*.

# Wagon Full of W's

Set out a wagon. Let the children look around the room to find objects whose names begin with the letter *W*. As they find each object, have them put it in the wagon. When the wagon is full, take out the objects one at a time, naming them as you go.

# Only for W

Have the children stand in a circle.
Ask them to listen carefully. If you ask them to do something that begins with W, such as *wiggle, wave, wink, wag, waltz, walk,* or *waddle,* have them do it. If, however, you ask them to do something that does not begin with *W,* such as *run, gallop, smile,* or *clap,* have them stand still.

## Phonics

# Xx

## X's on X's

Give each child an *X*-shape cut out of construction paper. Let the children use markers or crayons to write *X's* all over their letter shapes. Or give them toothpicks and let them glue the toothpicks in the shape of *X's* all over their letters. When they are finished, hang their *X's* all around your room.

## X Marks the Spot

For each child, put a small treasure, such as a sticker or a pencil, in an envelope. Write an *X* on the outside of each envelope. Hide the envelopes around the room. Tell the children that on a treasure map, *X* marks the spot where the treasure is hidden. Explain that there are many treasures hidden in your room, and that the only way to find them is to look for the *X's*. As the children find the *X* envelopes, let them open them up to discover their treasures.

## Make an X

Write *X's* and other letters on index cards. Have the children sit in a circle. Show them how to make the letter *X* with two index fingers. Hold up the letter cards one at a time. Whenever you hold up an *X* card, have the children make *X's* with their fingers.

*Hint:* Instead of writing letters on index cards, use the alphabet card patterns on pages 74–80 to make the letter cards for this activity.

## Box of X's

Find a large box and cover it with construction paper. Let the children use markers and crayons to write upper- and lowercase *X's* all over the box.

## Kisses and Hugs

Draw several *O's* on a sheet of plain paper and make copies for the children. Let the children add an *X* next to each *O* to make a page of kisses and hugs. (Explain to the children that *X's* and *O's* are sometimes written like that to mean kisses and hugs.)

## Exercise for X

Have the children listen as you name several words with the *X* sound in them. Point out that the *X* sound is sometimes found near the beginning of the word (*exit, examine, extra*) and sometimes at the end of the word (*box, fix, ax*). Let the children think of an exercise they would like to do, such as jumping jacks or running in place. Have them listen carefully. Whenever they hear a word with the *X* sound in it, have them do their exercises.

## X Song

Sing the following song with the children. Have them make *X's* with their fingers whenever they hear a word with an *X* sound.

Sung to: "If You're Happy and You Know It"

There's a fox in my box, in my box.
There's a fox in my box, in my box.
There's a fox in my box,
And I think he's eating lox.
There's a fox in my box, in my box.

There's a six in my mix, in my mix.
There's a six in my mix, in my mix.
There's a six in my mix,
That I'm not sure I can fix.
There's a six in my mix, in my mix.

There's some wax on my ax, on my ax.
There's some wax on my ax, on my ax.
There's some wax on my ax,
And I'm not being lax.
There's some wax on my ax, on my ax.

## Phonics

# Yy

## Yellow Y's

Give each child a *Y*-shape cut out of yellow construction paper. Set out decorating materials in yellow such as paper, fabric, ribbon, yarn, poms, sequins, buttons, and beads. Let the children glue the decorating materials onto their letter *Y*-shapes. When the glue is dry, hang their completed letters all around your room.

## Y's in the Yard

Make twenty photocopies of the *Y* alphabet card pattern on page 80. Cut out the cards and hide them all around your yard. Let the children go outside to find the *Y's* in the yard.

## Yodeling Y's

Write *Y's* and other letters on index cards. Teach the children how to yodel. Let them practice several times. Then hold up the letter cards one at a time. Whenever the children see a *Y* card, have them yodel.

 *Hint:* Instead of writing letters on index cards, use the alphabet card patterns on pages 74–80 to make the letter cards for this activity.

# Yarn Y's

Cut yarn into short pieces. Set out the yarn, small bowls of glue, and paintbrushes. Give each child a sheet of construction paper. Have the children brush glue all over their papers. Show them how to arrange the yarn on their papers to make upper- and lowercase Y's.

 *Variation:* Use only yellow yarn for this activity.

# Y's for the Yacht

Use yarn or yardsticks to make the outline of a yacht on the floor. Set out small squares of paper and pencils. Have the children write their own Y tickets in order to board the yacht. Put up a sign to indicate what combination of upper- and lowercase Y's you would like on the tickets. For example, you could ask them to write tickets with Yy, YY, yy, or yY.

# Yes or Yawn

Have the children listen carefully as you say a word. Ask them to yell out, *Yes!*, if the word starts with the letter Y. Have them yawn if the word does not begin with Y. Repeat with a variety of words.

# The Sound of Y

Sing the following song with the children. Let them take turns thinking of words that begin with Y to substitute for the word *yogurt*.

Sung to: "The Muffin Man"

The sound of Y is yuh-yuh-yuh,
Yuh-yuh-yuh-yuh, yuh-yuh-yuh-yuh.
The sound of Y is yuh-yuh-yuh,
Yuh-yuh as in yogurt.

# Phonics

# Zz

## Zoo Z's

Give each child a Z-shape cut out of construction paper. Let the children decorate their Z shapes with pictures of zoo animals. These can be zoo animal stickers, prints made from zoo animal rubber stamps, or even small pictures of zoo animals cut out of nature magazines. When the children are finished, hang their zoo Z's all around your room.

## Zigzag Z's

Write two columns of Z's on a sheet of plain paper. Laminate the paper (or cover it with clear self-stick paper). Let the children take turns using a black crayon to draw zigzag lines back and forth between the columns, connecting all the Z's.

## Zip for Z's

Write Z's and other letters on index cards. Ask the children to wear zippered coats or sweaters to school. While the children are still wearing their zippered coats or sweaters, show the letter cards to them one at a time. Have the children zip their coats and sweaters up and down whenever you show them a Z letter card.

*Hint:* Instead of writing letters on index cards, use the alphabet card patterns on pages 74–80 to make the letter cards for this activity.

## Zebra Z's

Cut sheets of white and black construction paper into quarters. Give each child a quarter sheet of each color. Have the children use black crayons to write upper- and lowercase Z's on the white paper, then give them white crayons to write upper- and lowercase Z's on the black paper. Point out how their Z's look like zebra stripes.

## Z Zone

Cover a flat area of your room with butcher paper. This could be a table, a spot on the floor, a wall, or even the back of a bookcase. Set out a box of crayons by the paper. Explain to the children that this paper is the *Z Zone*. Whenever they walk by the *Z Zone*, they should stop and write an upper- and lowercase *Z* on the paper. Move the *Z Zone* paper to different spots around your room.

## You Belong in the Zoo

Have the children pretend to be zookeepers. Collect a variety of stuffed animals and other objects. Hold up the animals and objects one at a time. If it is something that belongs in the zoo (one of the stuffed animals), have the children say, *Zoo.* If it is something that does not belong in the zoo, have the children say, *Zilch.*

## Zoom for Z

Recite the following rhyme with the children. Let them think of other words that begin with *Z* to substitute for *zany, zoo, zucchini, zebra, zipper,* and *zither.*

Zoom for the Z words,
Zoom for the Z words,
Zoom for the Z words,
Stop!

Zany, zoo, zucchini,
Zebra, zipper, zither.

Zoom for the Z words,
Zoom for the Z words,
Zoom for the Z words,
Stop!

## A to Z

Copy each of the alphabet letter cards on pages 74–80. Laminate the cards (or cover them with clear self-stick paper). Let the children work individually to arrange the cards in alphabetical order on a table. Or, give each child one or two of the alphabet cards. Have the children work together to place the cards in order on the floor.

 *Variation:* Put a magnet strip on the back of each card and let the children arrange them on a large metallic surface, such as a file cabinet or a refrigerator.

## Alphabet Concentration

Make two photocopies of the alphabet letter cards on pages 74–80. Laminate the letters (or cover them with clear self-stick paper). Select several pairs of letter cards and turn them facedown on a table. Invite two or three children to play *Alphabet Concentration*. Have the first child turn over two of the cards. If the cards match, the child keeps the cards and turns over two more cards. If the cards do not match, the child turns them facedown again and his or her turn is over. Then the next child has a turn. Continue taking turns until all of the letter pairs have been found.

 *Hint:* Vary the number of letter pairs you have, depending on the children's skills. Use fewer cards in the beginning as the children are learning this game. Add more letter pairs as the children's skills increase.

## Alphabet Books

Make a copy of all of the alphabet letter cards on pages 74–80 for each child. (Be sure to include the "My Alphabet Book" card and the "Now I've sung my ABC's, won't you sing along with me?" card.) Let the children cut out the cards and arrange them in order with the "My Alphabet Book…" card as the front cover and the "Now I've sung…" card at the back of their books. Help the children staple their books together, and have them write their names on the fronts. Let them color the inside pages, if you wish. Then have the children take their alphabet books home to read to their families.

# Phonics

## In the Alphabet

Sing the following song with the children. At the end of the song, say the alphabet together.

Sung to: "The Wheels on the Bus"

There are 26 letters in the alphabet,
The alphabet, the alphabet.
There are 26 letters in the alphabet,
Can you say them now?

## I Love the Alphabet

Set out the alphabet cards from the "A to Z" activity on page 58. Sing the first verse of the following song with the children. At the end of the verse, choose one child to find and hold up his or her favorite alphabet card. Sing the second verse of the song about that letter. Repeat the second verse for each child, or as many times as you like.

Sung to: "The Farmer in the Dell"

I love the alphabet.
I love the alphabet.
From *Z* to *A* and *A* to *Z*
I love the alphabet.

I love the letter _____.
I love the letter _____.
It's the best from *A* to *Z*.
I love the letter _____.

 Phonics

## Letter Collages

Decide what kind of letter collages you would like the children to make. Do you want them to make a collage for a specific letter? Or do you want them to make a collage with all of the alphabet letters? Give each child a sheet of construction paper. Tell the children what letters they will be looking for in the magazines, newspapers, junk mail, and catalogs you have set out. Let them look through the materials to find the selected alphabet letters. Have them cut out the letters and glue them to their papers.

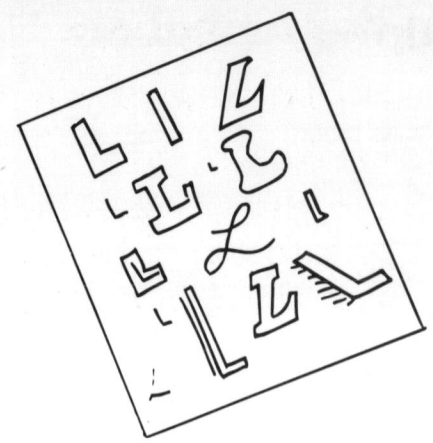

## Alpha-Ball

Use a permanent marker to write alphabet letters on a plastic ball. Have the children sit in a circle with you. Hold onto the ball and say, *A*. Then roll the ball to one of the children. Have that child say, *B* and roll the ball to another child. Continue until you have said the whole alphabet together.

 *Hint:* To make the game more challenging, start with a letter other than *A*.

## Make-Your-Own Alphabet Books

Over the course of the year, let the children make pages for their own alphabet picture books. For each letter, have them write the letter in upper- and lowercase at the top of a plain sheet of paper. Let them find magazine pictures of objects whose names begin with that letter to glue onto the page. Keep each child's pages in a separate file folder. At the end of the year, put each child's letters together to make his or her very own alphabet book.

 *Variation:* Instead of making individual books, let the children work together to create a class alphabet book.

## Alphabet Towers

Collect a set of alphabet blocks. Let the children take turns building alphabet towers with the blocks. Have the children name all of the letters in their towers.

*Variation:* Draw up simple blueprints for building alphabet towers. For example, you could show the *A*, *D*, and *G* blocks on the bottom, with the *H* and *M* blocks on top of them, followed by the *W* block. Have the children take turns building alphabet towers to specifications.

## Typing Letters

Find an old typewriter to set up in your room. Have plenty of plain paper on hand. Show the children how to use the typewriter. Let them take turns using it to type lots and lots of letters. Have the children name the letters as they type. Or, let them read the letters to you when they are finished.

## Letter Stencils

Purchase a set of letter stencils (available at office supply stores). Show the children how to place a stencil on a sheet of paper and color over it or trace around it with a crayon. Or show them how to set the stencil on the table, place a sheet of plain paper on top of it and rub an unwrapped crayon over it to make a letter rubbing. Encourage the children to use the stencils to write their names and other familiar words.

## Phonics

### Modeling Clay Letters

Give each child a handful of modeling clay. (Purchase modeling clay in a large tub or mix up a batch of your own. See recipe that follows.) Show the children how to roll the clay into "snakes," then form the snakes into alphabet letters. Let the children make as many different letters as they can with their clay.

> Modeling clay—Mix together 2 cups flour, 1 cup salt, 1 tablespoon vegetable oil, and 1 cup water. Add food coloring as desired.

*Variation:* Have the children flatten their modeling clay with rolling pins and use alphabet cookie cutters to cut letters out of the dough.

### Salt Writing

Cover the bottom of a 9" x 13" baking pan with salt. Let the children take turns using their fingers to write in the salt. Show them how to gently shake the pan to "erase" their letters. Let them write and erase as many letters as they like.

*Variation:* Instead of salt, use cornmeal or sand.

### Fingerpaint Letters

Cover a table with butcher paper. Put several spoonfuls of fingerpaint on the butcher paper. Have the children put on aprons and roll up their sleeves. Then let them use their hands to spread out the fingerpaint. Show them how to use their fingers to write letters in the paint and then how to make the letters disappear by smoothing out the paint with their hands.

# Chalkboard Fun

Set out a small chalkboard and some chalk. (You can purchase chalkboards at toy and school supply stores.) Invite one of the children to join you. Explain that you are going to be writing upper- and lowercase letters together. For example, if you write an uppercase *F* on the chalkboard, have the child write a lowercase *f*. If you write a lowercase *r*, have the child write an uppercase *R*. Begin with letters the child knows, moving on to more difficult letters. If needed, very lightly write the child's letter on the chalkboard for him or her to trace over.

 *Variation:* Have two chalkboards available, one for you and one for the child, while playing this game.

# Fill in the Blanks

Make this write-on, wipe-off alphabet game for the children. On a plain sheet of paper, write a row of five letters, leaving off one of the letters. For example, you could write *F G __ I J*. Repeat with several other rows of letters, writing some rows in uppercase and others in lowercase. Laminate the paper (or cover with clear self-stick paper). Let the children take turns using a black crayon to fill in the blanks with the missing letters. Show them how to wipe off the crayon with a dry paper towel.

# Back and Forth

Attach a plain sheet of paper to a clipboard. Invite one of the children to join you. Write the letter *A* on the paper, pass the clipboard to the child, and have him or her write the next letter of the alphabet. Continue back and forth until you have written the whole alphabet together.

 *Variation:* Instead of writing the whole alphabet, write one letter and have the child write the letter that comes after it. Then write a different letter and have the child write the letter that comes before it.

## Phonics

### Roll a Category

Find a small cube and cover each side with construction paper. Glue a magazine picture to each side of the cube to represent one of the following categories: food, animals, vehicles, toys or games, jobs, and places. Collect the alphabet cards from the "A to Z" activity on page 58. Pass out the most common letters, such as *S, T, R, L, N, E,* and *A,* to the children. Let one child roll the cube. Help the child name the category that is on the top. Have each child think of something that begins with the letter he or she is holding and that belongs in the category. For example, if the category is animals, and the child is holding the letter *T,* he or she could say *tiger* or *turtle*. Let each child have a chance to name something in the category. Have the children exchange letter cards before rolling the cube again.

### Letters to My Friends

Set up a mini-office for the children to use to write letters to their friends. Have paper, envelopes, postcards, rubber stamps, pens, pencils, paperclips, and other supplies available. Make a list of all the children's names and hang it up in the office. Encourage the children to write notes and letters to one another. Set up cubbies or mailboxes for delivering the children's messages.

### Letters Around the Room

Give the children removable sticky notes and pencils. Have each child choose an object, write the first letter of its name on a sticky note, and place the note on the object. Then walk around the room with the children looking for their notes. When you find one, sing the following song together, substituting the name of the letter for *T* and the name of the object for *table*.

Sung to: "The Farmer in the Dell"

There are letters around the room
Letters around the room
Look I see
A *T* by me
On the table in the room.

# Alphabet Minis

Set up a miniature alphabet cabinet to give the children lots of opportunities for hands-on alphabet exploration. Purchase a multi-drawer cabinet at a hardware or craft store. Label each drawer with a different alphabet letter. Invite children and their parents to help you fill the drawers of the cabinets with miniature objects. Try to have several objects for each letter's drawer. Here are some suggestions:

A—apple, alligator, ambulance
B—ball, bell, bow
C—cow, candle, cat
D—dinosaur, dish, domino
E—egg, elf, envelope
F—fish, feather, football
G—goldfish, guitar, gift
H—hammer, horse, hat
I—igloo, insect, instrument
J—jeep, jewel, jet
K—kite, key, kangaroo
L—lion, ladybug, leaf
M—magnet, mitten, motorcycle
N—nut, newspaper, necklace
O—octopus, olive, octagon
P—pumpkin, penguin, pickle
Q—quilt, quill, quarter
R—rabbit, ribbon, ruler
S—sock, sunflower, sailboat
T—teddy bear, toothbrush, ticket
U—umbrella, unicorn, uniform
V—violin, valentine, van
W—waffle, worm, walrus
X—x-ray, box, fox
Y—yo-yo, yacht, yarn
Z—zebra, zipper, zinnia

# Stamping Through the Alphabet

Collect alphabet rubber stamps and rubber stamps featuring objects that begin with each letter of the alphabet. Many craft stores have an extensive selection of rubber stamps, including animals, foods, and nature objects. Let the children use the alphabet stamps to make alphabet cards, alphabet books, and alphabet pictures.

## Phonics

# Letter Sound Song

Sing the following song with the children. Let them think of new words and letters to substitute for *cat* and *C*.

Sung to: "Mary Had a Little Lamb"

> Cat begins with the letter *C*,
> The letter *C*, the letter *C*.
> Cat begins with the letter *C*.
> Cuh-cuh-cuh-cuh cat.

### A for Apple

Sung to: "Twinkle, Twinkle, Little Star"

> *A* for apple, *B* for bear,
> *C* for cat and *D* for doll.
> *E* for elephant, *F* for fog,
> *G* for gate and *H* for hog.
> *I* for igloo, *J* for jam,
> *K* for kite and *L* for lamb.

> *M* for music, *N* for nail,
> *O* for ox and *P* for pail.
> *Q* for quiet, *R* for rose.
> *S* for sail and *T* for toes.
> *U* for upstairs, *V* for vest,
> *W, X, Y, Z* are the rest.

# Sign Language Alphabet

Teach the children the sign language alphabet. As they are learning the letters, repeat the name and sound of each one. This is a great way to combine sight, sound, and touch to reach your visual, auditory, and tactile learners.

 **Hint:** You can learn the sign language alphabet from books such as *The Handmade Alphabet* by Laura Rankin (Dial Books for Young Readers, 1991), *My First Book of Sign Language* by Joan Holub (Troll Associates, 1996), and *Signing at School* by S. Harold Collins (Garlic Press, 1992).

# Phonics

## Rhyme Patterns

**Teacher:** Use these patterns with the "Sound of A" activity on page 7.

## Phonics

**Cake Pattern**

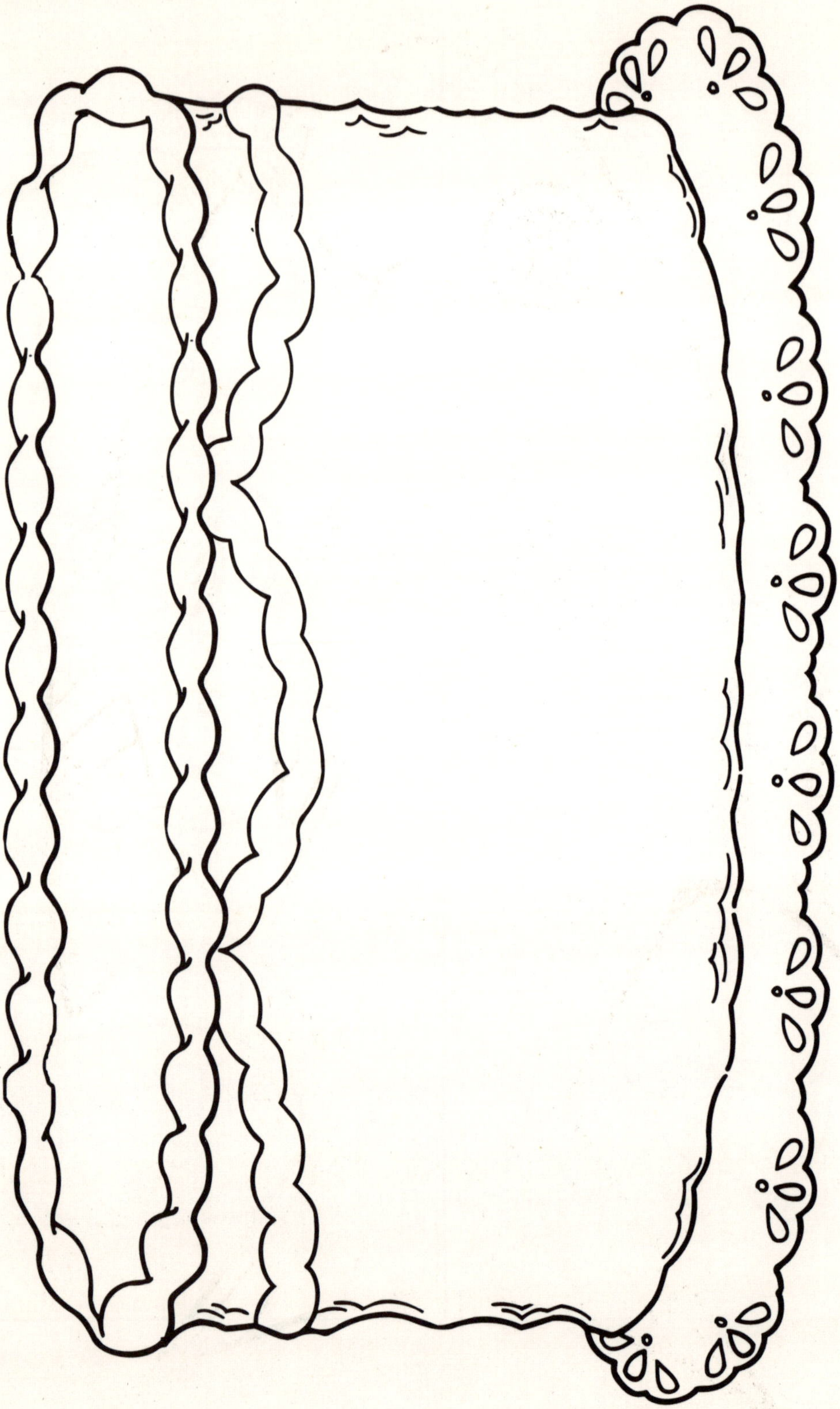

**Teacher:** Use this pattern with the "Cute Cakes" activity on page 11.

## Fish Pattern

Phonics

**Teacher:** Use this pattern with the "Fish F's" activity on page 16.

Phonics

# Kite Pattern

**Teacher:** Use this pattern with the "K Kites" activity on page 27.

## Laundry Pattern

**Teacher:** Use this pattern with the "L Laundry" activity on page 28.

Phonics

## Sailboat Pattern

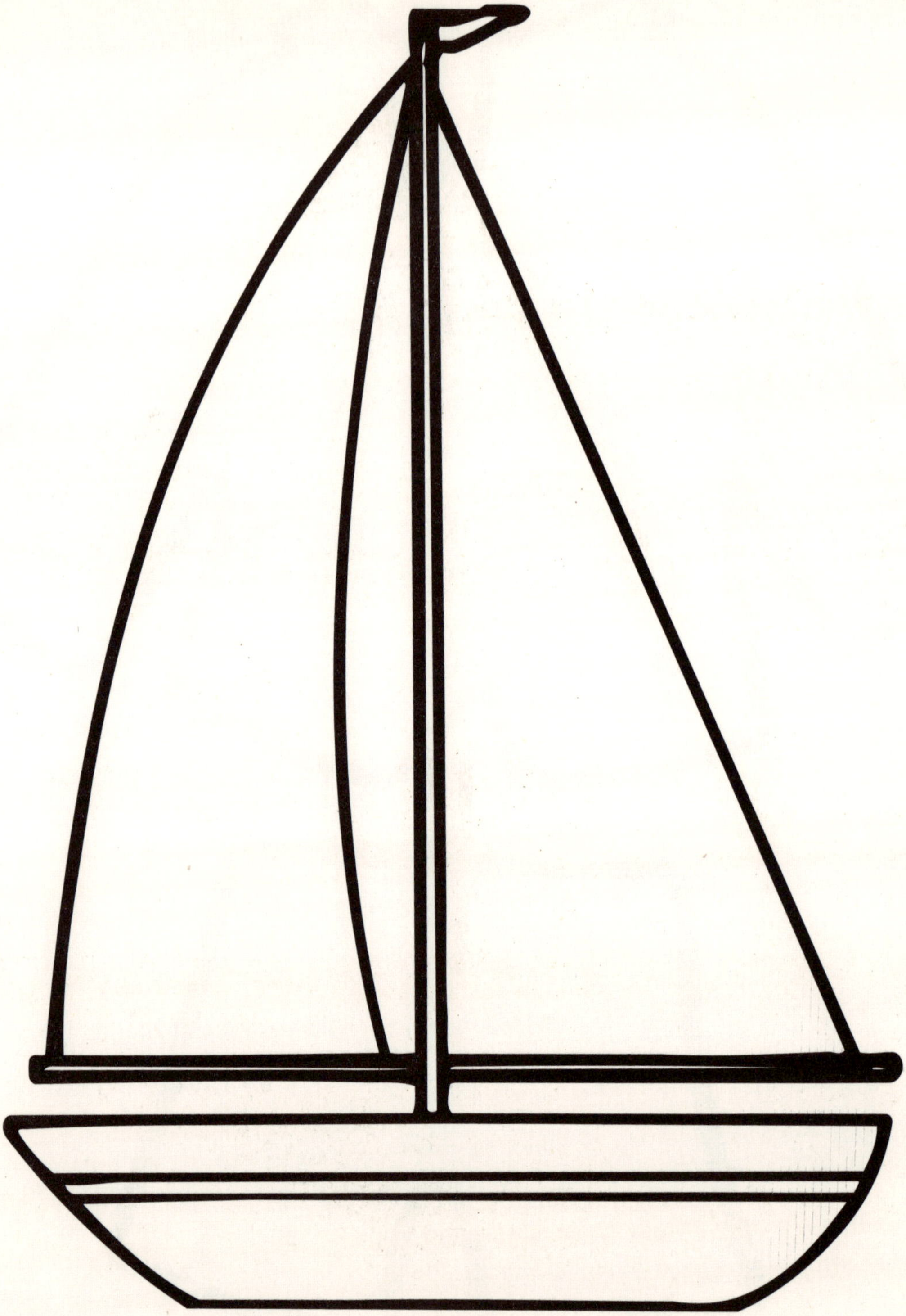

**Teacher:** Use this pattern with the "Sea of S's" activity on page 43.

# Umbrella Pattern

Phonics

**Teacher:** Use this pattern with the "Umbrella U's" activity on page 47.

## Phonics

### Alphabet Card Patterns

alligator

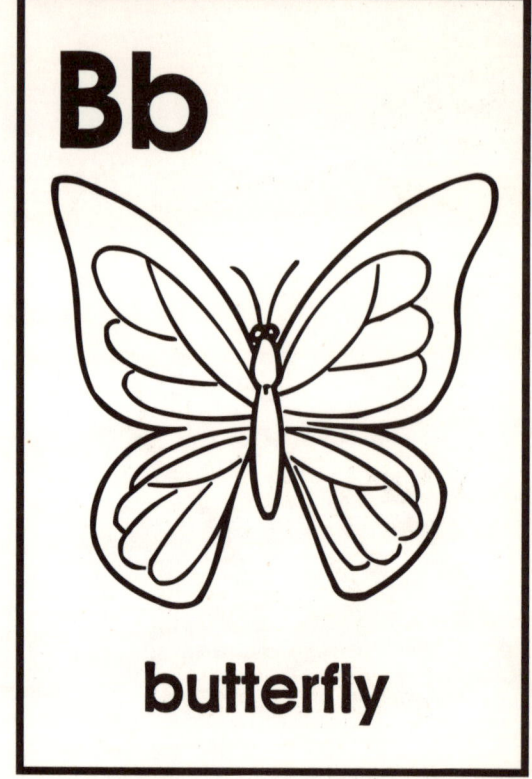

butterfly

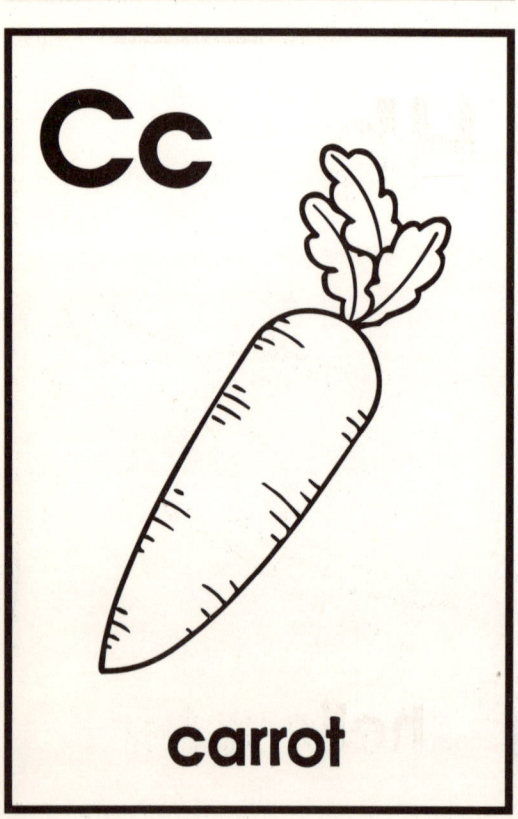

carrot

door

---

**Teacher:** Use these patterns with activities throughout the book.

# Alphabet Card Patterns

Phonics

elephant

feather

goat

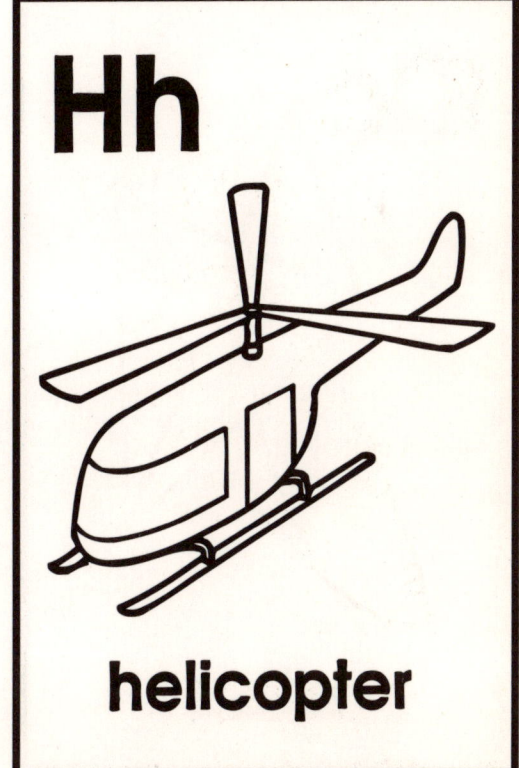
helicopter

**Teacher:** Use these patterns with activities throughout the book.

## Phonics

**Alphabet Card Patterns**

igloo

jeep

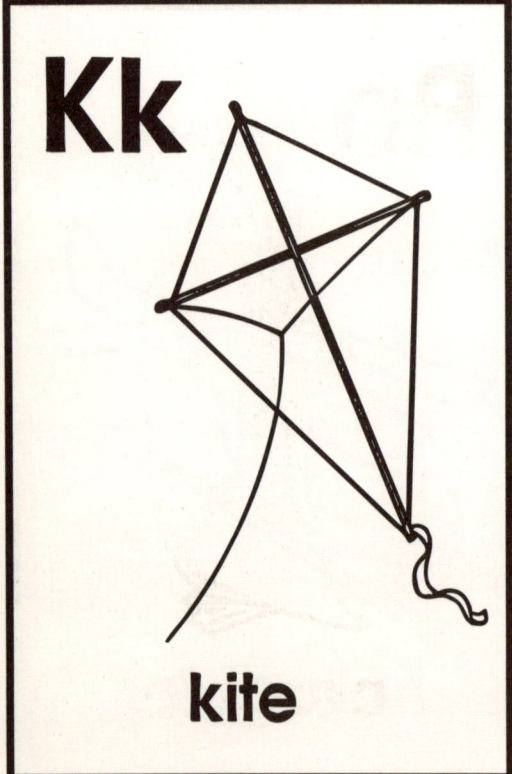

kite

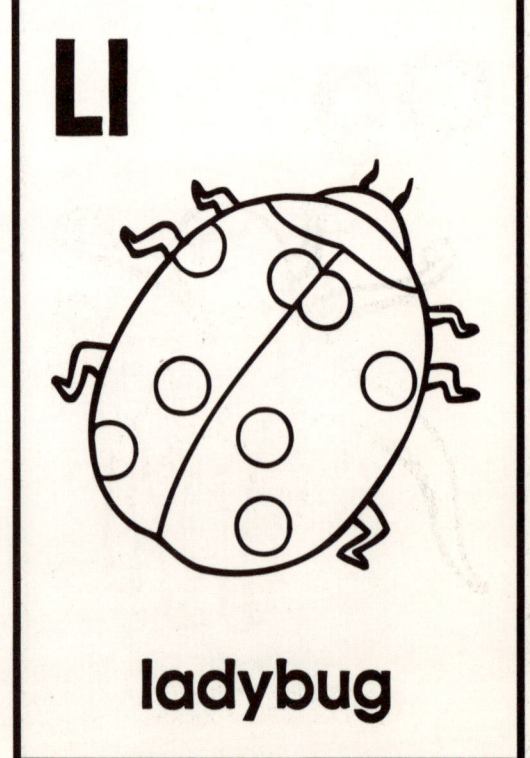

ladybug

**Teacher:** Use these patterns with activities throughout the book.

Phonics

## Alphabet Card Patterns

mailbox

newspaper

octopus

penguin

**Teacher:** Use these patterns with activities throughout the book.

**Phonics**

## Alphabet Card Patterns

quarter

raccoon

sailboat

tiger

**Teacher:** Use these patterns with activities throughout the book.

# Alphabet Card Patterns

Phonics

**Uu**
umbrella

**Vv**
violin

**Ww**
wagon

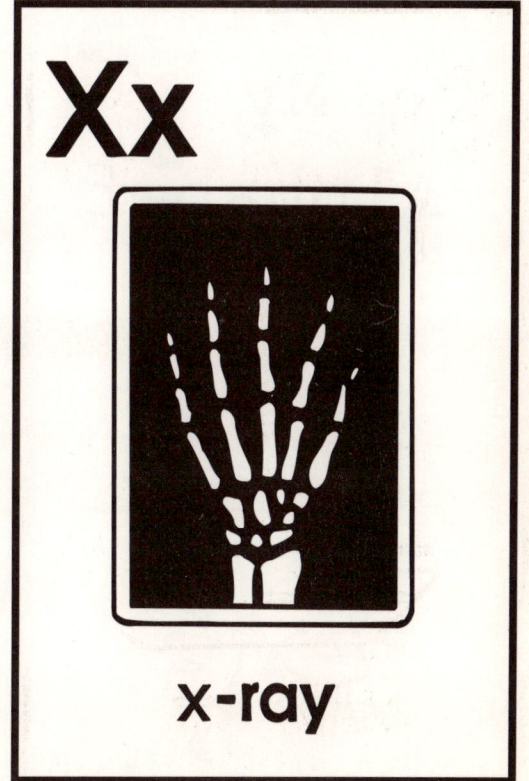
**Xx**
x-ray

**Teacher:** Use these patterns with activities throughout the book.

 **Phonics**

## Alphabet Card Patterns

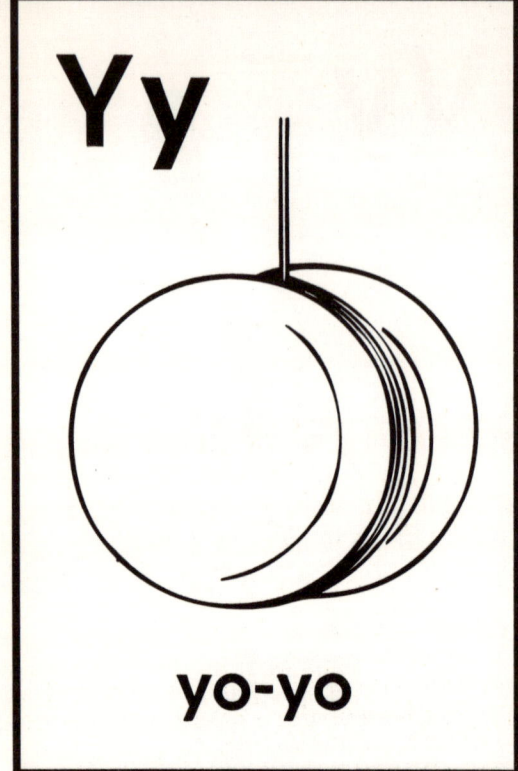

yo-yo

zebra

My Alphabet Book

Name: _____

Now I Know

My ABC's.

Next time won't you

sing with me?

---

**Teacher:** Use these patterns with activities throughout the book.